D1513204

PUZZLE QUEST

secret island

Written & illustrated
by Kia Marie Hunt

Published by Collins
An imprint of HarperCollins Publishers
HarperCollins Publishers
Westerhill Road
Bishopbriggs
Glasgow G64 2QT

www.harpercollins.co.uk

HarperCollins Publishers
Macken House, 39/40 Mayor Street
Upper Dublin 1, D01 C9W8, Ireland

10 9 8 7 6 5 4 3

© HarperCollins Publishers 2022
Collins® is a registered trademark of HarperCollins Publishers Limited

ISBN 978-0-00-853210-9
Printed and bound in the UK using 100% renewable electricity
at CPI Group (UK) Ltd

All rights reserved. No part of this book may be reproduced, stored in a retrieval
system, or transmitted in any form or by any means, electronic, mechanical,
photocopying, recording or otherwise, without the prior permission in writing
of the Publisher.

The contents of this publication are believed correct at the time of printing.
Nevertheless the publisher can accept no responsibility for errors or omissions,
changes in the detail given or for any expense or loss thereby caused.

A catalogue record for this book is available from the British Library.

Publisher: Michelle l'Anson
Author and Illustrator: Kia Marie Hunt
Project Manager: Sarah Woods
Designer: Kevin Robbins

MIX
Paper | Supporting
responsible forestry
FSC™ C007454

This book is produced from independently certified FSC™ paper
to ensure responsible forest management.

For more information visit: www.harpercollins.co.uk/green

PUZZLE QUEST

secret island

Written & illustrated
by kia Marie Hunt

It's a blustery day when you find the dotty balloon. It has blown across the sea to you on a warm breeze.

All tied up with some kind of exotic vine, the balloon carries with it a scroll and a shiny old compass.

You unravel the scroll to find a map and a scrap of paper that reads:

'FOLLOW THE COMPASS TO SECRET ISLAND & FIND DODOSS'

'Dodoss...?' Could that mean 'dodos?' As in... the bird species that has been extinct for over 300 years!?

Could dodos really still be alive today, hiding in a secret faraway location?

There's only one way to find out...

Let the adventure of discovery begin.
Be ready to explore long-forgotten worlds
and solve more than 100 fun puzzles,
collecting clues along the way!

Things you'll need:

* **This book**
* **A pen or pencil**
* **Your amazing brain**

That's it!

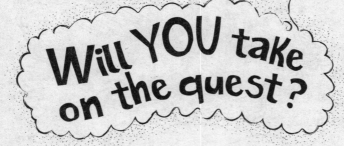

Will YOU take on the quest?

**Psssst!
Always look out for
this telescope symbol:**

This means you've found a clue.

Write down all the clues you find
in your Clue Logbooks
(on pages **30, 54, 78, 102** and **126!**)

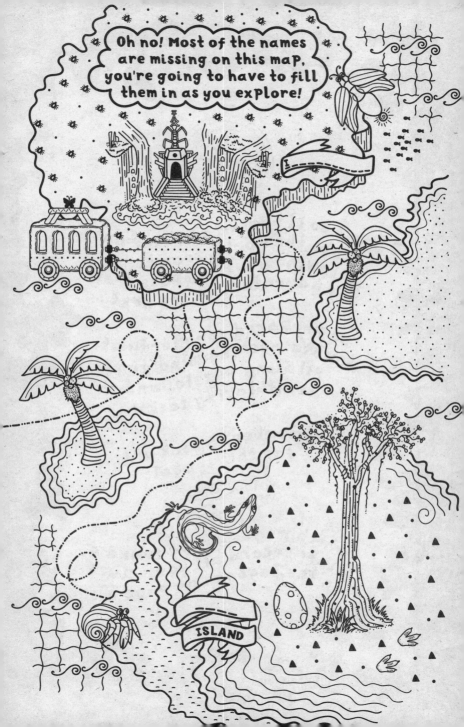

And so it begins. You step out
into the world, soon to be
following your compass from
one adventure to the next...

Be prepared for plenty of
mountaineering mind games,
piloting puzzles and
trailblazing tasks!

Remember to look out
for this symbol:

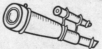

which means you've found a
clue! Record all your clues
in the logbook on Page 30.

Who knows what you'll encounter on this adventure!? Make sure you pack your explorer's kit with everything you might need on your epic journey.

BACKPACK

BINOCULARS

BOOTS

COMPASS

MAP

NET

SNACKS

TORCH

Can you find all the words from the
list on the opposite page in the
wordsearch below? Words may
be hidden horizontally or vertically.

T	A	A	G	O	A	J	Q	T	G	V
R	U	E	W	B	I	Q	J	O	S	P
T	E	T	M	A	P	U	B	R	C	X
G	R	P	P	C	Q	T	O	C	O	A
U	P	X	L	K	E	C	O	H	M	T
P	T	R	L	P	P	P	T	R	P	S
S	L	C	Z	A	W	A	S	K	A	N
B	I	N	O	C	U	L	A	R	S	A
M	Y	I	E	K	S	E	L	R	S	C
C	R	A	J	N	E	T	S	C	R	K
D	W	U	O	Q	S	R	C	T	R	S

Every great explorer needs a great exploring stick to take with them on their treks.

Which silhouette correctly matches your new exploring stick? Circle your answer.

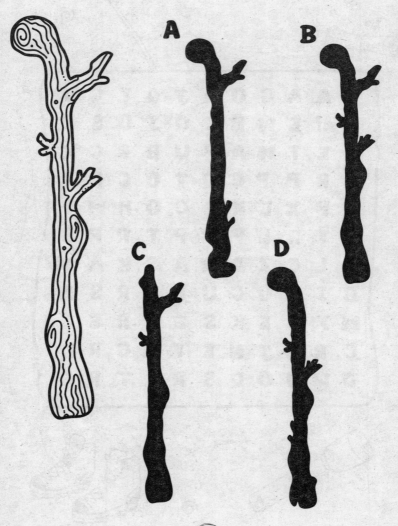

A

B

C

D

As you follow the compass, you're glad you packed a spare pair of boots! The journey takes you up slopes, down valleys, across streams and through some very squelchy muddy puddles...

Follow the tangled paths. Which one leads you all the way to the Mysh Hills? Write your answer into this box.

W   X   Y   Z

The Mysh Hills

The Mysh Hills are very big and you spend so much time climbing that you begin to feel tired. You start to look for somewhere to set up camp.

Can you make your way through the Mysh Hill maze all the way to the forest in the centre?

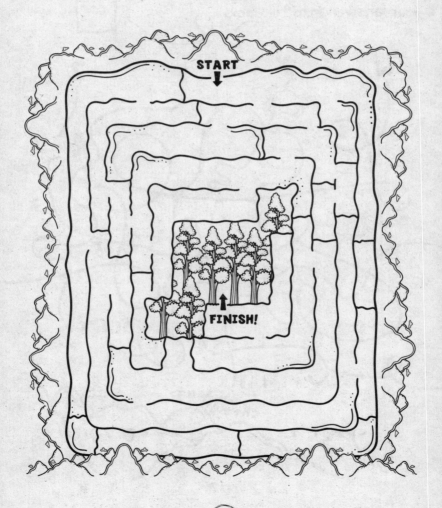

Solve the number problem below each letter in the Key. Then use the answers to fill in the gaps in the story below. The first one has been done for you.

A 2+3 | B 10-8 | C 6×2 | D 35÷5 | E 18÷7 | H 10×3 | M 8÷2 | N 4×2

5

O 30÷2 | P 20-6 | R 2×9 | S 9÷3 | T 16-6 | U 12-6

AS YOU ENTER THE FOREST,

YOU FIND A _ _ A _ G _ _ A _ _
5 3 10 18 5 8   25 3 30 5 14 25

ON THE G _ _ _ _ _ . YOU DON'T
18 15 6 8 7

KNOW WHAT I_ I_ , BUT IT
10   3

FEELS I _ _ _ _ _ A _ _ SO YOU
4 14 15 18 10 5 8 10

_ _ _ IT IN YOUR _ A _ K _ A _ K.
14 6 10   2 5 12 14 5 12

In the forest, you find a campsite but all of the tents are empty and some of them even look a bit like they have been trampled on...

Solve the sudoku puzzles as you inspect the tents.

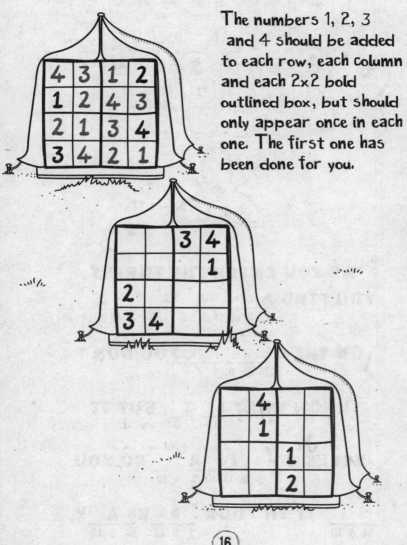

The numbers 1, 2, 3 and 4 should be added to each row, each column and each 2x2 bold outlined box, but should only appear once in each one. The first one has been done for you.

In the word-wheels, find three outdoor words.
Each word starts with the centre letter and uses
all the letters in the wheel once.

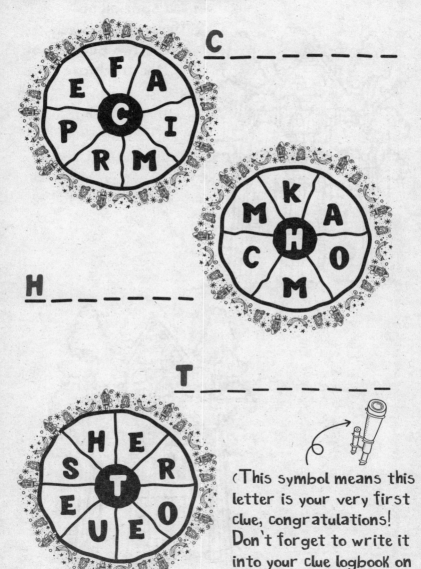

C _ _ _ _ _ _ _

H _ _ _ _ _ _ _

T _ _ _ _ _ _ _

(This symbol means this
letter is your very first
clue, congratulations!
Don't forget to write it
into your clue logbook on
page 30!)

You leave the tents and decide to climb up and stay the night in a cosy treehouse instead!

Can you spot all six differences between these two pictures of the treehouse?

As you step inside, you notice clues that make you think someone, or something, is already staying in this treehouse...

Make your way from start to finish. You can move up, down or sideways but you can't move diagonally and you must follow the clues in this order:

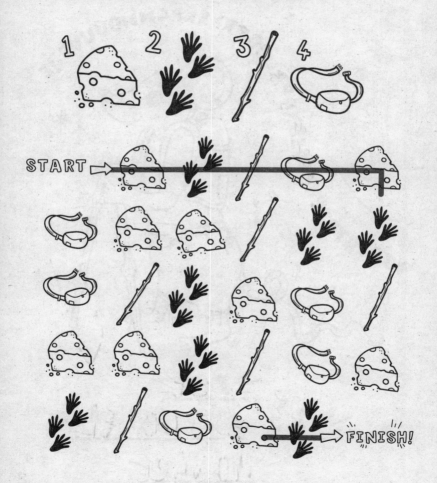

Who is this? Let's find out...

Scribble out every other letter from left to right. Write the letters that are left over on the lines below. The first two letters have been scribbled out for you.

the JET EXPLORER MOUSE

This new friend has a poem for you!

Follow the lines and write the letter from each circle into the space at the end of each line to fill in the gaps.

Did you know that
　　　Mysh means MOUSE ?

What brought you
　　　to this tree HOUSE ?

Our meeting was
　　　surely meant to BE,

Exploring fills
　　　me up with GLEE !

Shall we let
　　　this story UNRAVEL ?

May I come with
　　　you on your TRAVELS ?

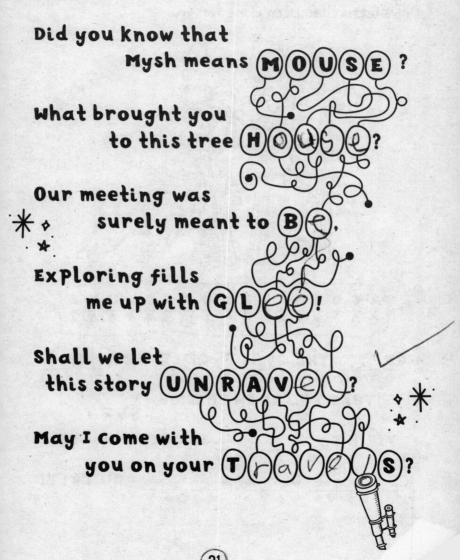

Oh no, the next morning you are rudely awoken by what feels like an earthquake!

Use the symbol key to crack the code and fill in the gaps to reveal more about what's happening. The first letter has been done for you.

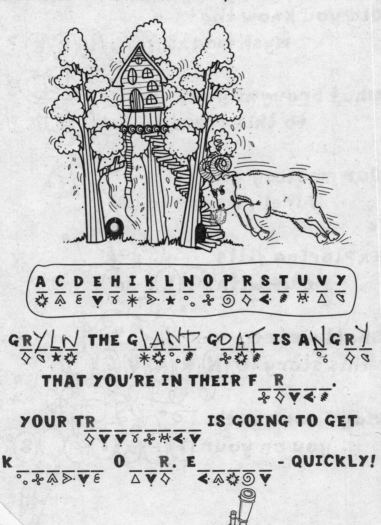

A	C	D	E	H	I	K	L	N	O	P	R	S	T	U	V	Y
✿	◈	ℰ	▽	⅄	✳	▷	★	°	⌘	◎	◇	◀	⚡	⋇	△	◊

GR̲Y̲L̲N̲ THE G̲I̲A̲N̲T̲ GO̲A̲T̲ IS AN̲G̲R̲Y̲

THAT YOU'RE IN THEIR F_R___.

YOUR TR_____ IS GOING TO GET

K_____ O___ R.E_____ - QUICKLY!

Run! Don't forget to pop Jet into your pocket because their little legs won't carry them fast enough!

Follow the numbers across each hanging bridge from left to right and figure out which number is next in the sequence. Write the final number into the circle at the end of each bridge.

The bridges take you to a runway high up in the trees, with four planes to choose from.

Complete the number problems below and write your answers into the boxes. Each plane should have the same answer. The odd one out is the plane you take off in, but which one is it?

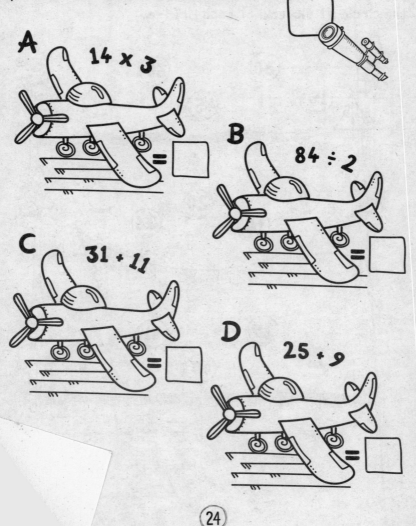

A   14 x 3   =

B   84 ÷ 2   =

C   31 + 11   =

D   25 + 9   =

Phew! That was a lucky escape...

The numbers 1, 2, 3 and 4 should be added to each row, each column and each 2x2 bold outlined box, but should only appear once in each one. The first one has been done for you.

You have a great view as you fly over the Mysh Hills with your new friend.

So far, you've hiked on foot and flown in a plane – you begin to wonder what other kinds of transport you'll use while on this adventure...

3 letters
BUS
CAR

4 letters
SHIP
TAXI
TRAM

5 letters
HORSE
MOPED
TRAIN
YACHT

6 letters
SLEDGE

7 letters
BICYCLE

10 letters
HELICOPTER
SKATEBOARD

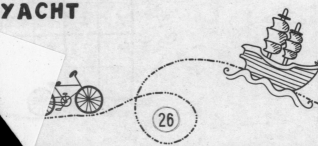

Place each of the transport words from the list on the opposite page into the empty squares to create a filled crossword grid. Each word is used once so cross it off the list as you place it to help you keep track.

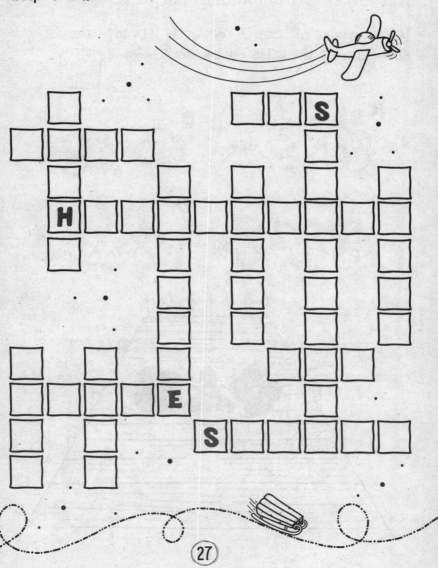

The compass leads your plane to an empty dock with three strangely shaped holes on it. The shape you found fits perfectly into one of the holes. Jet the mouse says they also collected two shapes like this that they found in the hills!

Which order of shapes correctly fits into the silhouette of the holes on the dock below?

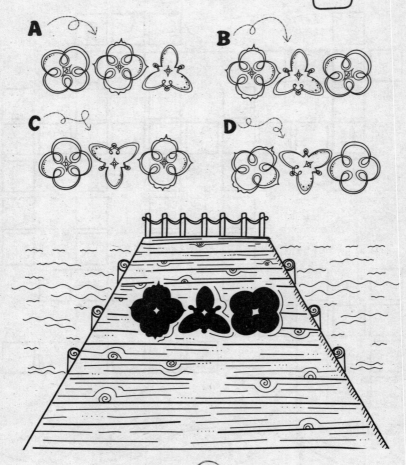

The moment you fit all three shapes into place, something large rises up next to the dock from underneath the water... what is it?

Cross out any letter that appears more than once in the grid below. Write the letters that are left over on the lines below in the order they appear, and a hidden word will reveal itself. Letter D has been scribbled out to start you off.

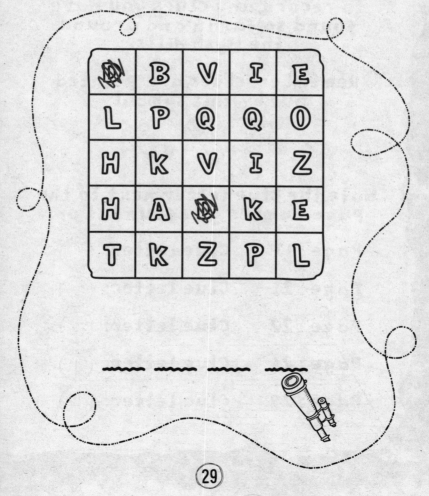

~~D~~	B	V	I	E
L	P	Q	Q	O
H	K	V	I	Z
H	A	~~D~~	K	E
T	K	Z	P	L

___ ___ ___ ___

CLUE LOGBOOK:
The Mysh Hills

Before you and Jet get on the boat to continue your adventure, take a minute to use this logbook to record any clues you have found so far in and around the Mysh Hills.

Remember, clues are pointed out by this symbol:

Note the clue letter next to the page number you found it on:

Page : 17   Clue letter: ◯

Page : 21   Clue letter: ◯

Page : 22   Clue letter: ◯

Page : 24   Clue letter: ◯

Page : 29   Clue letter: ◯

NOTES

(Blank 'notes' pages like this are handy
for jotting down any notes or working
out when you're busy solving puzzles!

You could also use them
to write, doodle or
anything else you'd
like to do while on
your quest!)

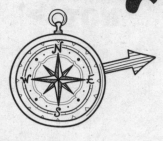

You cross a wide lake until you reach an island. Could this be the 'secret island' mentioned in the note?

You and Jet brought the plane AND the boat with you, just in case. But it looks like you won't be needing the plane here – the trees are too dense to see anything from above (or to land amongst!).

As you sail upriver, be ready for some forest-floor number fun, creature word quests and party game puzzles!

As you sail up the island's wild, overgrown river, it begins to get narrower, until your boat is too big for it!

Can you sail through the maze from start to finish, making sure you pass through the centre to hop off your boat and onto the wooden raft?

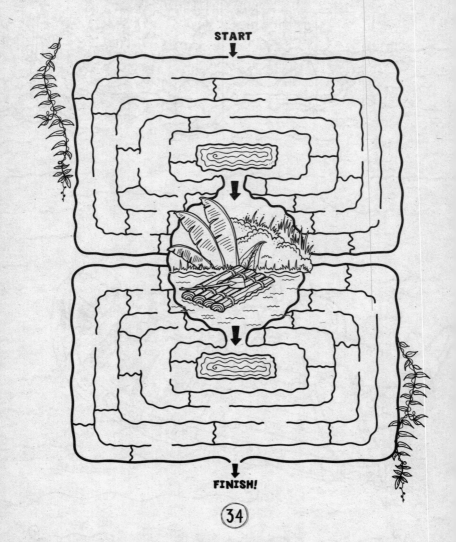

START

FINISH!

Cross out any letter that appears more than
once in the grid below. Write the letters that
are left over on the lines below in the order they
appear, and a hidden word will reveal itself.
Letter Q has been scribbled out to start you off.

Q̶	J	I	S	S
Z	Q̶	H	D	Z
U	K	N	X	Z
I	H	G	L	P
P	D	E	X	K

IT LOOKS LIKE THIS
ISLAND IS ONE HUGE

___ ___ ___ ___ ___ ___

After sailing through endless wilderness, your compass begins to point away from the river...

It's time for you to get off the raft and explore the jungle on foot. Jet travels in your pocket again – you don't want them to get lost in the undergrowth!

3 letters
WET

6 letters
CANOPY
LAUREL

4 letters
PALM
VINE
WARM

8 letters
RAINFALL
ROSEWOOD

5 letters
GREEN
MOIST

9 letters
EVERGREEN
TEMPERATE

Place each of the jungle words from the list on the opposite page into the empty squares to create a filled crossword grid. Each word is used once so cross it off the list as you place it to help you keep track.

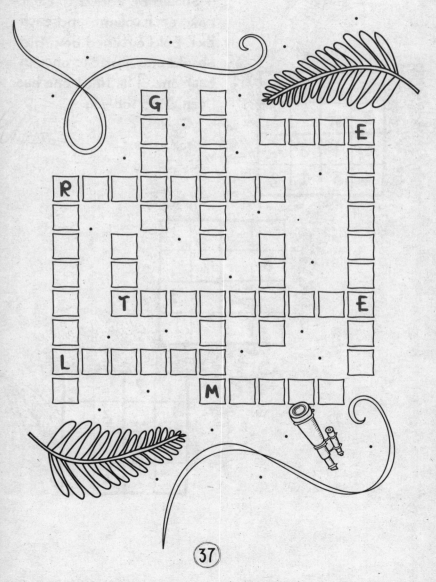

The jungle is thick with trees, the floor covered in plants, leaves and vines – watch where you step!

The numbers 1, 2, 3 and 4 should be added to each row, each column and each 2x2 bold outlined box, but should only appear once in each one. The first one has been done for you.

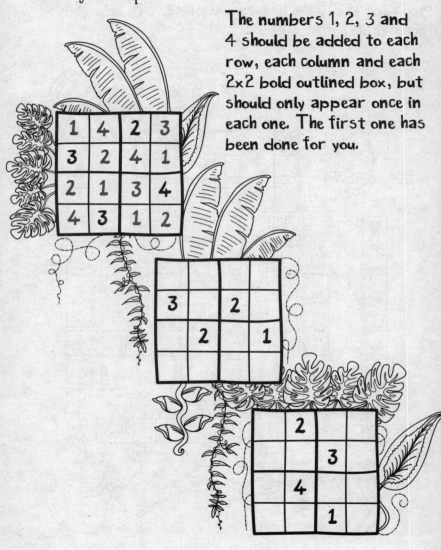

You discover a scary-looking sign warning of the creatures who live here, but you must keep following the direction of the compass...

Use the grid references to work out each letter and reveal the name on the sign. The first letter has already been done for you.

As you trek deeper into the jungle you realise
the Tree Terrors are all around, watching you...

Hide and seek: How many pairs of eyes can you see
watching you in this picture of the jungle?
Write your answer in the box.

Can you escape them by swinging away on vines?

Follow the numbers up each of the hanging vines and figure out which number is next in the sequence. Write the final number into the circle at the top of each vine.

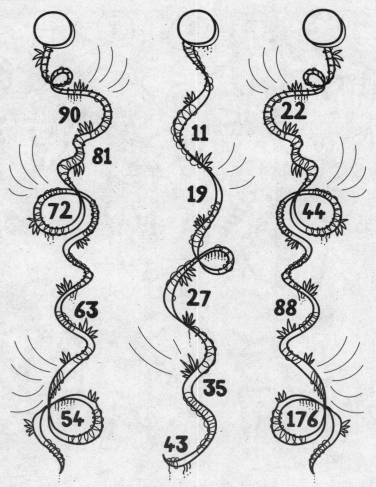

90
81
72
63
54

11
19
27
35
43

22
44
88
176

Uh oh! They're catching up to you...

Well that's a surprise and a relief! The Tree Terrors aren't terrifying after all. They're like a cross between jaguars and lemurs... they're actually quite adorable!

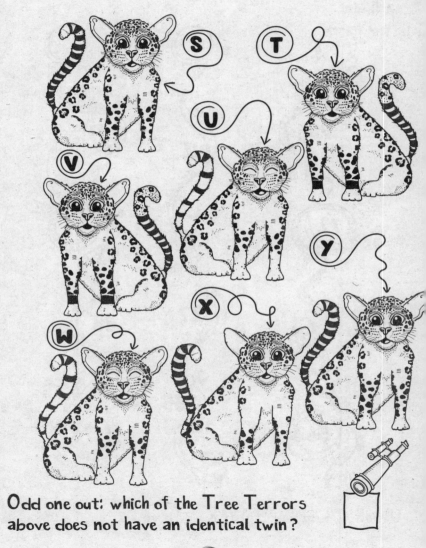

Odd one out: which of the Tree Terrors above does not have an identical twin?

The Tree Terrors are very friendly, they don't suit their name at all! You show them your compass and tell them about your quest to find dodos.

Solve the number problem below each letter in the Key. Then use the answers to fill in the gaps. One letter has been done for you.

You agree to help by going to find the other jungle creatures and spread the word that the Tree Terrors aren't as scary as they sound. Off you venture, in the opposite way to where the compass has been leading you...

Which of the tangled jungle paths will take you back to the river so you can cross over it? Write your answer in the box.

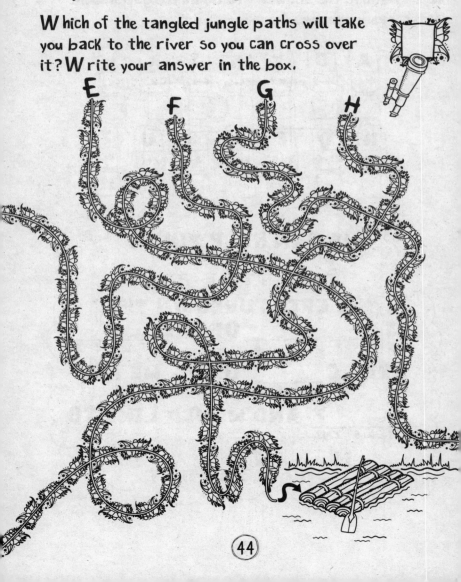

On the way you decide to change the sign so it looks less scary. You give the Tree Terrors a new, friendly name that suits them better.

Use the grid references to work out each letter and reveal the new name you put on the sign. The first letter has already been done for you.

Once you cross the river, you soon notice how much more alive the other side of the jungle is. There are so many creatures here, including lots of butterflies!

Can you find all the butterfly names from the list on the opposite page in the wordsearch below? Words may be hidden horizontally or vertically.

```
P W M L D X S E C L E
E W S T G M W S H R T
A S R M O N A R C H W
C G L R L R L G R N A
O A S T A C L Y K T E
C O I P R W O E E W L
K E B L U E W I N G R
Y J C L I Q T A C D O
M E A D O W A U G T S
W L O N G W I N G A S
A D M I R A L G K R T
```

ADMIRAL

BLUEWING

LONGWING

MEADOW

MONARCH

PEACOCK

SWALLOWTAIL

You meet lots of other animals on this side of the island. Hopefully you can invite them over to be friends with the lonely 'Tree Chums'.

Which silhouette correctly matches each jungle creature? Circle your answers.

In the word-wheels, find three big jungle cats. Each word starts with the centre letter and uses all the letters in the wheel once.

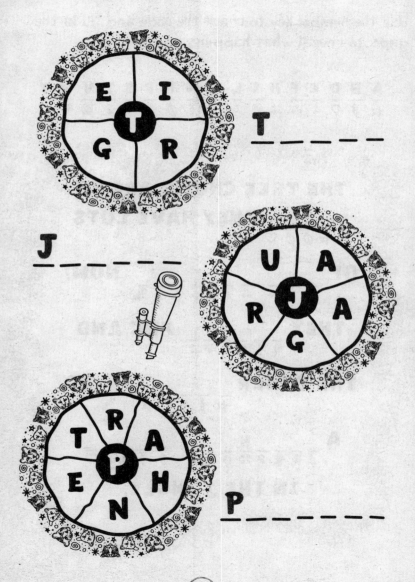

T _ _ _ _

J _ _ _ _ _

P _ _ _ _ _ _

The animals from the other side of the jungle agree to come with you to meet the Tree Chums after you explain how nice they really are.

Use the symbol key to crack the code and fill in the gaps to reveal what happens next...

A B D E F H I L M N P R S T V W Y

(symbol key below each letter)

THE TREE CHUMS ARE SO

H _ _ _ _   **THEY HAVE LOTS**

OF _ _ _ _ _ _ _   **NOW!**

THEY _ _ _ _ _ _   **YOU AND**

THE OTHER _ _ _ _ _ _ _   **TO**

A _ _ _ _ _ **H** _ _ _ _ _ _

IN THE JUNGLE.

Make your way from start to finish. You can move up, down or sideways but you can't move diagonally and you must follow the jungle party items in this order:

1   2   3   4

START

FINISH!

One of these party animals has something they want to tell you...

Complete the number problems below and write your answers into the boxes. Each animal should have the same answer. The odd one out is the animal you talk to, but which one is it?

A   6 × 3   =☐

B   38 ÷ 2   =☐

C   54 ÷ 3   =☐

D   15 + 3   =☐

As the animal approaches you, you think about how you haven't seen any dodos so far on your adventure.

The compass has led you through the island, and is now pointing across a vast ocean...

Scribble out every letter J. Write the letters that are left over on the lines below to reveal a message from the animal on the opposite page. The first one has been done for you.

JTJHAJJNJJKJYJOUFOJRJ
YJOUJRJHJELPJYOJUJCAJN
JUJSJEOUJRSJHJIPJTO
JCJROJSJSTJHEJJOCJEJAJN

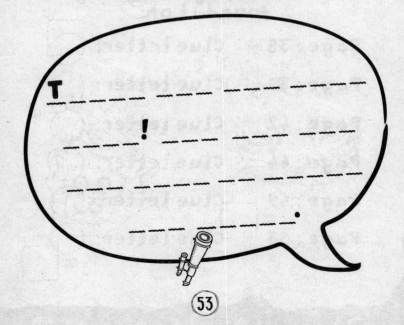

T___ ___ ___ ____
___ ! ___ ___ ___
___ ___ ___ ___
___ ___ ___.

CLUE LOGBOOK: Jungle Island

Tonka the Tree Chum would also like to come along for the rest of your adventure... the more the merrier!

Before you hop onto the ship, make a note of all the clues you found on Jungle Island.

Remember to note the clue letter next to the page number you found it on:

Page : 35   Clue letter: ◯

Page : 37   Clue letter: ◯

Page : 42   Clue letter: ◯

Page : 44   Clue letter: ◯

Page : 49   Clue letter: ◯

Page : 53   Clue letter: ◯

★ NOTES ★

Well, that was certainly a secret island, but you didn't find dodos... maybe there is more than one island?

As you cross this vast ocean with Jet and your new friend Tonka the Tree Chum, you notice that the compass is doing something you didn't think was possible... it's pointing straight down!

Are you ready for some watery word puzzles, nautical number fun and marine mysteries?

In the middle of this vast ocean, you sail up to a sign that points straight down into the water!

Use the symbol Key on the left to crack the code and reveal what the sign says. The first letter has been done for you.

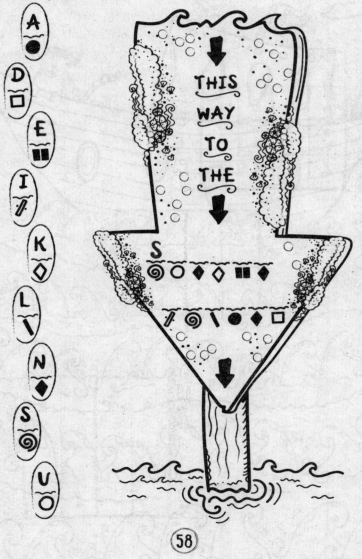

THIS WAY TO THE

S U N K E N

I S L A N D

Before you can explore underwater, you must complete these sea sudoku puzzles.

The numbers 1, 2, 3 and 4 should be added to each row, each column and each 2x2 bold outlined box, but should only appear once in each one. The first one has been done for you.

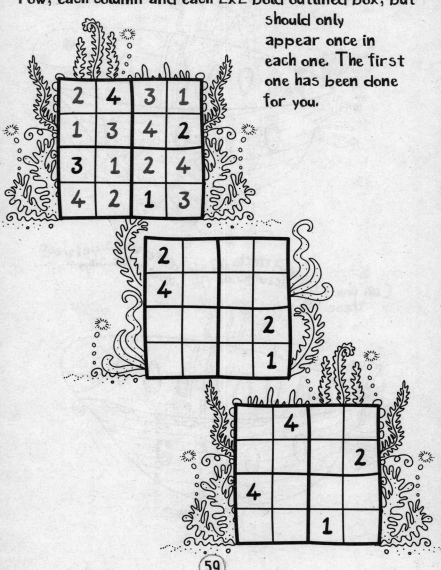

At the push of a few buttons, your ship converts into a submarine that looks like a big fish! Perfect for the deep dive expedition you're about go on.

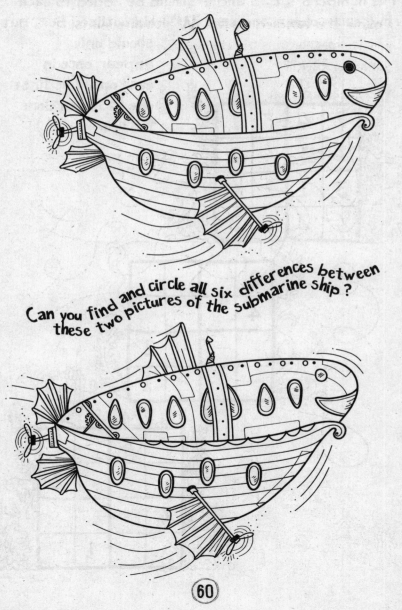

Can you find and circle all six differences between these two pictures of the submarine ship?

You, Jet and Tonka the Tree Chum set off into the deep ocean, using your ship submarine's telescope to search for the sunken island.

Follow the tangled paths. Which one leads you from the sign all the way down to the sunken island?

You've never travelled down to such depths
before, who knew the ocean was quite so deep!?

The words 'DEEP SEA' have been hidden together
in the grid below. Can you find the complete words?
The words may be hidden horizontally or vertically.

E E E D D E D S
A D A E E E D D E
E P A E E S E E E
A A D E E D S E A
E E E D E D D P S
D E E E A D E S E
S D A A E P S E S
A A E A P E A A S
E D S E D P D E D

The coral reef on this sunken island is teeming with life. You discover unidentified sea creatures, prehistoric fish and even two-headed seahorses!

Which silhouette correctly matches each sea creature? Circle your answers.

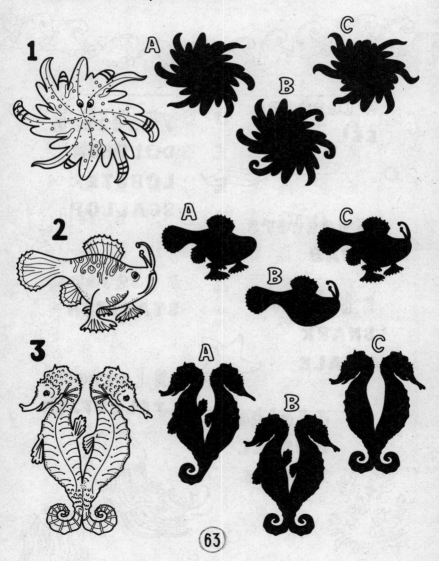

It's an amazing experience to discover a sunken island full of so many sea creatures, and to see them all up close. But you know that dodos won't live down here... so why has the compass led you underwater?

3 letters
EEL

4 letters
CRAB

5 letters
SHARK
WHALE

6 letters
MUSSEL
TURTLE

7 letters
DOLPHIN
LOBSTER
SCALLOP

8 letters
STARFISH

9 letters
JELLYFISH

Place each of the sea creature words from the list on the opposite page into the empty squares to create a filled crossword grid. Each word is used once so cross it off the list as you place it to help you keep track.

Suddenly, you notice something shiny floating up ahead... it's another of those strange shapes like the ones you and Jet found in the Mysh Hills!

Can you sail through the maze from start to finish, making sure you pass through the centre to collect the shape on your way?

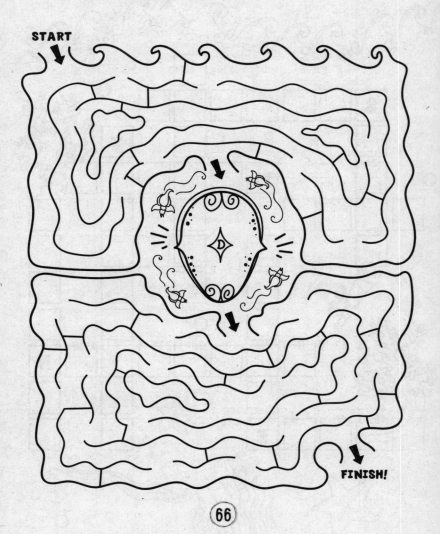

START

FINISH!

Oh no! You collect the shape with your submarine's grabbing tool, but what happens next doesn't exactly go to plan...

Solve the number problem below each letter in the Key. Then use the answers to fill in the gaps and reveal what happens. One letter has been done for you.

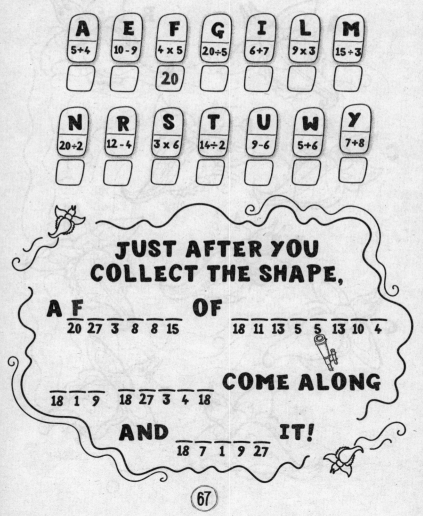

A	E	F	G	I	L	M
5+4	10-9	4 x 5	20÷5	6+7	9 x 3	15÷3
		20				

N	R	S	T	U	W	Y
20÷2	12-4	3 x 6	14÷2	9-6	5+6	7+8

JUST AFTER YOU COLLECT THE SHAPE,

A F _ _ _ _ _   OF _ _ _ _ _ _ _ _
  20 27 3 8 8 15   18 11 13 5 5 13 10 4

_ _ _ _ _ _ _ _   **COME ALONG**
18 1 9 18 27 3 4 18

AND _ _ _ _ _ **IT!**
       18 7 1 9 27

Quick, chase after those sea slugs!

Odd one out: which of these 'Sea Angel' slugs does not have an identical twin? That's the slug with the shape – the one you need to catch!

A

B

C

D

E

F

G

H

I

It's quite a chase, the sea slugs are small creatures but can swim surprisingly fast.

When you finally catch up to the sea slug with the shape, you tell them about your quest and ask if you can add the shape to your collection because it might be important...

Scribble out every letter **W** and letter **Z**. Write the letters that are left over on the lines below to reveal the sea slug's reply. The first one has been done for you.

WYZOUWCAWWNZHAWVEZTHWE
SHZZAPWEZIWFYZOUZCWAZW
ZLMZTWHEZCWAWTZFIWSZHW

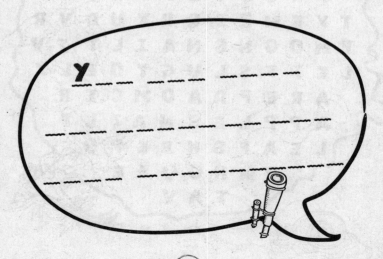

Y _ _ _ _ _ _

_ _ _ _ _ _ _ _

_ _ _ _ _ _ _ _

After meeting the many groups of different sea slugs and sea snails who live here, you find out that their neighbour (a huge catfish who is usually very relaxed and only eats algae) has recently become angry and is now threatening to eat them all!

Can you find all seven sea slug and snail names from the list on the opposite page in the wordsearch below? Words may be hidden horizontally or vertically.

```
        K O B
      T T O I L R E
      L S E A B U N N Y
      S E A A N G E L N E O
      F R O S T E D T R O R
      T Y E W Z I G R Y U D V R
      P M O O N S N A I L T J V
      L E P F S L U G T O E L Y
      A R E P A A O M C E R
      A P P L E S N A I L T
      L E A F S H E E P O
      R W H U U E E
        T A V
```

APPLE SNAIL

BLUE DRAGON

LEAF SHEEP

FROSTED

MOON SNAIL

SEA ANGEL

SEA BUNNY

You set off to find the catfish's lair. It's deep under the sunken island and it's dark down here. Only the glowing deep sea creatures can light the way.

Make your way from start to finish. You can move up, down or sideways but you can't move diagonally and you must follow the glowing jellyfish in this order:

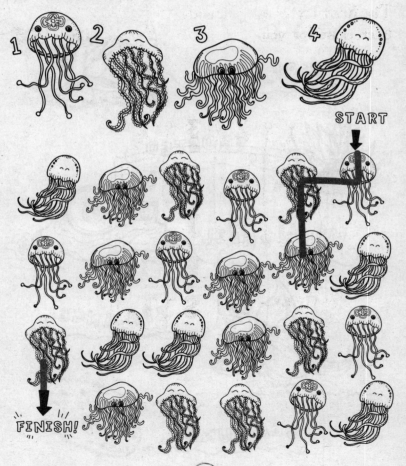

The catfish doesn't look happy to see you. It's much angrier and much more gigantic than you had hoped! This is one moody fish...

Use the grid references to work out each letter and reveal what is the matter with the catfish. The first letter has already been done for you.

	1	2	3	4
	A	K	Y	W
	H	N	J	C
	I	O	E	P
	R	U	S	T

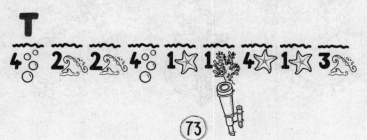

T _ _ _ _ _ _ _ _
4 2 2 4 1 1 4 1 3

Isn't it funny that one teeny tiny tooth is making this usually gentle giant so angry! You can help...

Follow the long and twisted ropes.
Which one is attached to the old anchor?

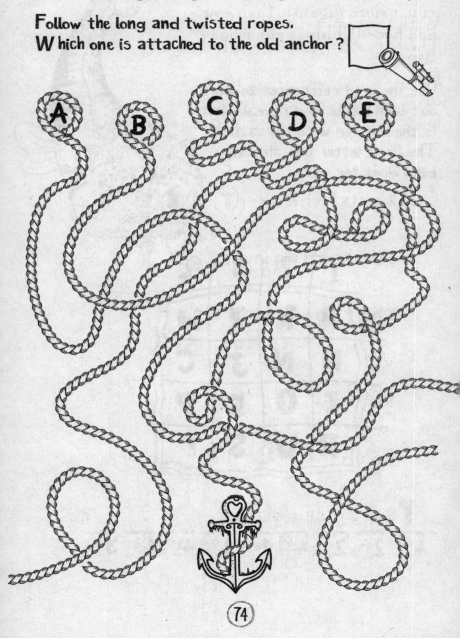

You tie the rope to the catfish's wobbly tooth, then drop the big anchor and... POP!

With a sigh of relief, out comes the tooth. The big catfish has a poem for you...

Follow the lines and write the letter from each circle into the space at the end of each line to fill in the gaps.

I must thank (T)(H)(E)(E) _____

for setting me (F)(R)( )( ) _____

That tooth and I,
did not (A)(G)( )( )( ). _____

I'm now ( )( )(P)(P)(Y) _____

to eat ( )(L)( )(A)( )... _____

Sorry sea slugs,
I'll leave you (B)( )! _____

Make your way from start to finish. You can move up, down or sideways, but you can't move diagonally and you must only follow the fish with even numbers in their lamps. The line has been started off for you.

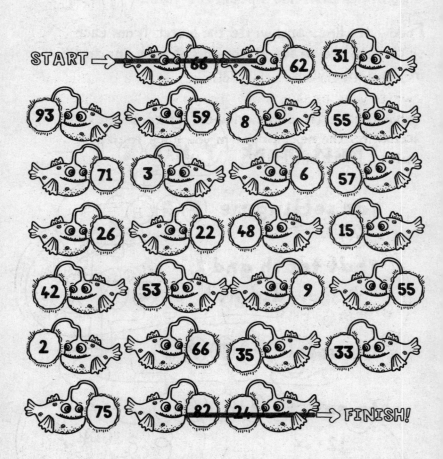

When you get back to the sea slug community, the catfish apologises and peace is restored. Everyone is very happy with you – they have even lovingly named you 'the deep-sea dentist'!

Your compass is now pointing back up towards the surface, so you decide to set off with Jet, Tonka and a new adventurous friend – Luca the Leaf Sheep.

But it's not that simple, now you have a new problem to deal with!

Complete the number problems in each bubble and write your answers into the circles. Each bubble should have the same answer. The odd one out contains the next problem you have to deal with... which one is it?

A
16 × 2
YOUR SUBMARINE HAS BROKEN DOWN!
=

B
60 - 26
A BIG SHARK IS COMING FOR YOU!
=

C
12 + 22
YOU GET CALLED HOME FOR DINNER!
=

D
17 × 2
TONKA SUDDENLY FEELS SEASICK!
=

CLUE LOGBOOK:
Sunken Island

Oh no! Your submarine ship may have broken down, but you don't need to worry too much...

The catfish is happy to help by towing you along until you reach your next destination!

Before you carry on, remember to record any clues you found on the Sunken Island.

Note the clue letter next to the page number you found it on:

Page : 65   Clue letter: ◯

Page : 67   Clue letter: ◯

Page : 69   Clue letter: ◯

Page : 73   Clue letter: ◯

Page : 74   Clue letter: ◯

✱ NOTES ✱

Towed along by a happy catfish, you and your new friends can now continue on your exciting journey!

The compass leads you to yet another island. You've almost forgotten that you're trying to find dodos because you're meeting so many weird and wonderful species!

Prepare yourself for some minibeast mysteries, winged word fun, tunnelling tasks and mantis mind games!

The first thing that catches your eye on this new island is a long train with carriages made of thick stone that looks so heavy, you can barely believe this train would ever be able to move!

Follow the lines and write the letter from each circle in the space at the end of each line to reveal a new word. Some letters have already been done for you.

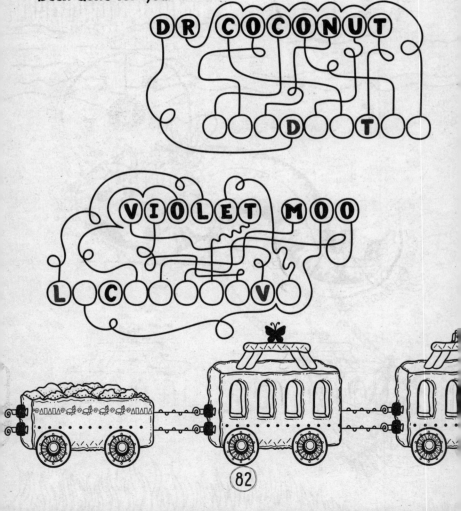

In the word-wheels, find three train words.
Each word starts with the centre letter and
uses all the letters in the wheel once.

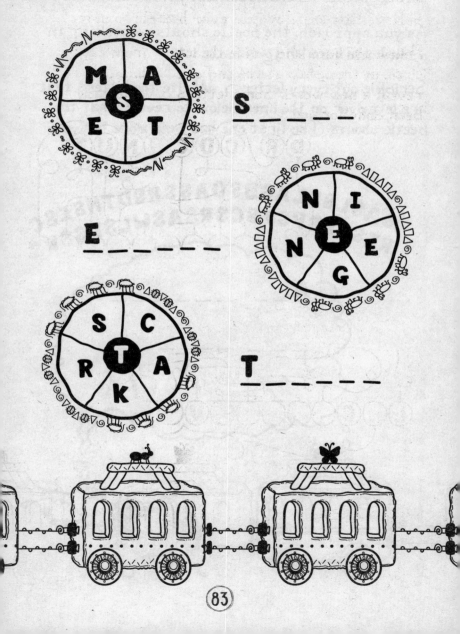

M A S E T

S _ _ _ _

N I N E E G

E _ _ _ _ _

S C T R A K

T _ _ _ _ _

You walk alongside the carriages to the front of this odd train, to find it is being pulled by a huge strong beetle with striped horns.

As you approach, the beetle shouts something in a loud and rumbling voice...

Scribble out every letter S. Write the letters that are left over on the lines below to reveal what the beetle shouts. The first one has been done for you.

SASLSSLASBSOASSRSDTHSESC
RESSESPSYSCSRSASWLSESSRS

A _ _   _ _ _ _ _ _

_ _ _   _ _ _ _ _ _

_ _ _ _ _ _ !

You and your friends hop aboard the train!

Follow the carriage numbers along each railway bridge from left to right and figure out which number is next in the sequence. Write the final numbers into the beetles.

25 22 19 16

27 34 41 48

62 56 50 44

This train is full of bugs, and no, there isn't an infestation... the bugs are the passengers!

A friendly ant informs you that you are travelling through the Lost Island of Insectopolis.

3 LETTERS
ANT

4 LETTERS
FLEA
GNAT
MOTH
WASP

5 LETTERS
LOUSE

6 LETTERS
BEDBUG
BEETLE
EARWIG

7 LETTERS
FIREFLY

8 LETTERS
CRANEFLY
HOVERFLY

11 LETTERS
GRASSHOPPER

Place each of the insect words from the list on the opposite page into the empty squares to create a filled crossword grid. Each word is used once so cross it off the list as you place it to help you keep track.

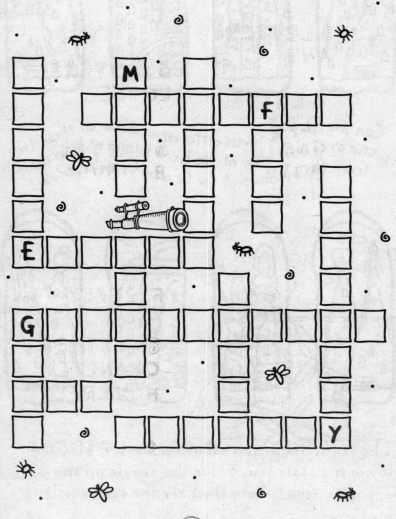

Can you spot all seven differences between these two pictures of your view of the Lost Island of Insectopolis from the windows of the Creepy Crawler train?

The train drops you off at the bottom of a towering staircase. Solve the puzzle on the opposite page to reveal where the stairs will lead you...

Cross out any letter that appears more than once in the grid below. Write the letters that are left over on the lines below in the order they appear, and a hidden word will reveal itself. Letter P has been scribbled out to start you off.

P	Y	Q	G	M
C	A	C	R	R
Y	K	N	Q	K
G	R	T	X	J
J	I	J	X	S

1,000 STEPS TO
THE TEMPLE OF THE

~~~ ~~~ ~~~ ~~~ ~~~ ~~~

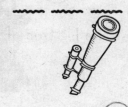

At the top of the staircase you reach an impressive view of a tall temple nestled between waterfalls.

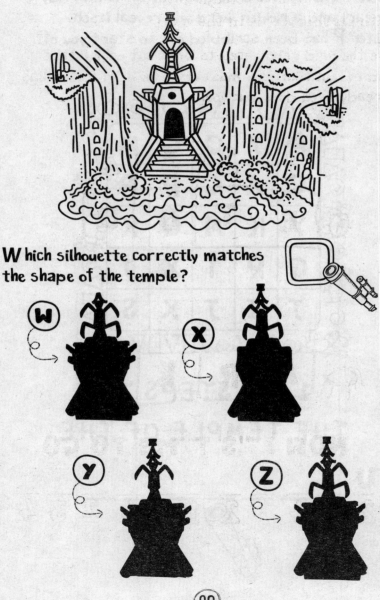

Which silhouette correctly matches the shape of the temple?

W

X

Y

Z

So you've climbed all the way to the top of 1,000 steps and you still can't get inside the temple!? It's very well protected... how will you get to it with all this water in the way?

Use the grid references to work out each letter and reveal what you must do. The first letter has already been done for you.

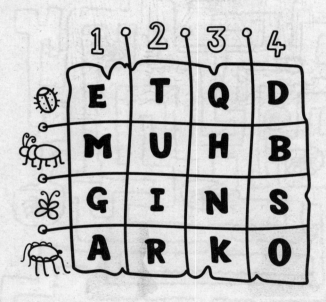

NOW IT'S TIME TO GO

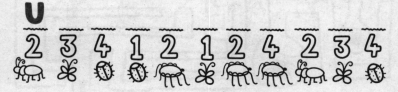

At the top of the steps you enter a tunnel network that takes you deep underground so you can pass under the water and into the temple from below.

Can you burrow like a bug down underground and through the maze from start to finish?

START

FINISH!

You finally make it to the temple, but you need to enter the right codes to open the gates and doors.

The numbers 1, 2, 3 and 4 should be added to each row, each column and each 2x2 bold outlined box, but should only appear once in each one. The first one has been done for you.

It is quite dark inside the temple. While you follow your compass through the long corridors, you can only see thanks to the soft glow of the fireflies and glow-worms inside.

Make your way from start to finish. You can move up, down or sideways, but you can't move diagonally and you must only follow the glowing insects with odd numbers. The line has been started off for you.

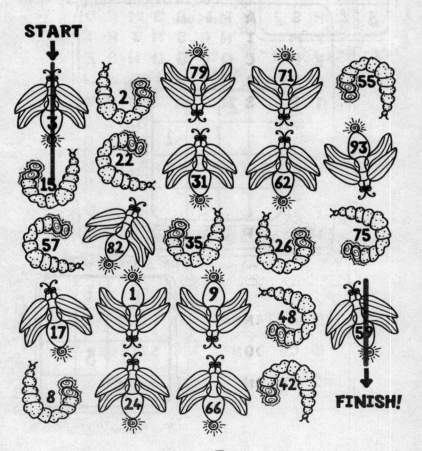

In the dim light you can see the walls of the temple are decorated with golden paintings of insects.

Can you find all eight insect words from the list in the wordsearch below? Words may be hidden in the grid horizontally or vertically.

```
H S W A R M B S M P D
Y M W I N G S N I R T
K R A C O C O O N O Z
I I R L H I V E A A W
T P C S A T A I S N K
J R O T U U C H Q T O
L V B I L A O L S E Q
K Q C N X I L E T N X
N H T G T O O G R N O
F Z E E R A N S X A O
W S W R R U Y S G E O
```

🐞 **ANTENNAE**   🐞 **LEGS**

🐞 **COCOON**   🐞 **STINGER**

🐞 **COLONY**   🐞 **SWARM**

🐞 **HIVE**   🐞 **WINGS**

Solve the number problem below each letter in the Key. Then use the answers to fill in the gaps and find out what happens in the temple. The first letter has already been done for you.

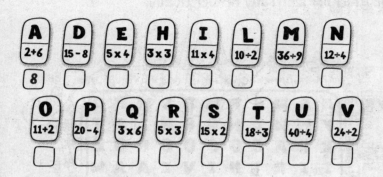

A	D	E	H	I	L	M	N
2+6	15-8	5x4	3x3	11x4	10÷2	36÷9	12÷4
8							

O	P	Q	R	S	T	U	V
11+2	20-4	3x6	5x3	15x2	18÷3	40÷4	24÷2

IN THE THRONE ROOM, YOU MEET

___ ___ ___ ___ ___   ___ **A** ___ ___ ___ **A** THE ___ **A** ___ ___ ___ ___ .
18 10 20 20 3   4 8 3 7 15 8   4 8 3 6 44 30

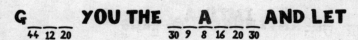

SHE SAYS SHE HAD A ___ ___ ___ ___ ___ ___
12 44 30 44 13 3

THAT TOLD HER SHE "SHOULD

G ___ ___ ___ YOU THE ___ **A** ___ ___ ___ AND LET
44 12 20   30 9 8 16 20 30

YOU GO". SO, SHE G ___ ___ ___ ___ YOU
44 12 20 30

TWO MORE ___ **A** ___ ___ ___ ___ ...
30 9 8 16 20 30

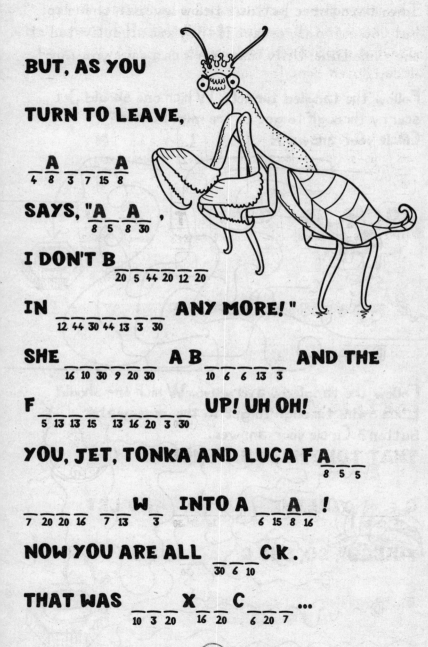

BUT, AS YOU

TURN TO LEAVE,

$\underset{4\ \ 8}{\text{A}}\ \underset{3\ \ 7\ \ 15}{\ }\ \underset{8}{\text{A}}$

SAYS, "$\underset{8\ \ 5}{\text{A}}\ \underset{8\ \ 30}{\text{A}}$,

I DON'T B $\underset{20\ \ 5\ \ 44\ \ 20\ \ 12\ \ 20}{\quad\quad\quad\quad}$

IN $\underset{12\ \ 44\ \ 30\ \ 44\ \ 13\ \ 3\ \ 30}{\quad\quad\quad\quad\quad}$ ANY MORE!"

SHE $\underset{16\ \ 10\ \ 30\ \ 9\ \ 20\ \ 30}{\quad\quad\quad\quad}$ A B $\underset{10\ \ 6\ \ 6\ \ 13\ \ 3}{\quad\quad\quad}$ AND THE

F $\underset{5\ \ 13\ \ 13\ \ 15\ \ 13\ \ 16\ \ 20\ \ 3\ \ 30}{\quad\quad\quad\quad\quad\quad}$ UP! UH OH!

YOU, JET, TONKA AND LUCA F $\underset{8\ \ 5\ \ 5}{\text{A}\ \ }$

$\underset{7\ \ 20\ \ 20\ \ 16\ \ 7\ \ 13}{\quad\quad\quad\quad}\ \underset{3}{\text{W}}\ $ INTO A $\underset{6\ \ 15\ \ 8\ \ 16}{\ \ \text{A}\ }$!

NOW YOU ARE ALL $\underset{30\ \ 6\ \ 10}{\quad\ }$ C K.

THAT WAS $\underset{10\ \ 3\ \ 20}{\quad\ }$ X $\underset{16\ \ 20}{\ }$ C $\underset{6\ \ 20\ \ 7}{\quad\ }$ ...

97

There are three buttons and a lever in the trap, but you can only escape if they are all activated at the same time. Only teamwork can save you now!

Follow the tangled tunnels. Which one should Jet scurry through to get to the mini button? Circle your answer.

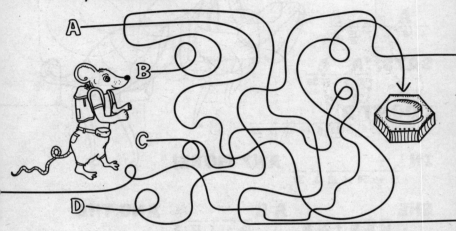

Follow the tangled waterways. Which one should Luca swim through to get to the underwater button? Circle your answer.

Follow the tangled ropes. Which one should Tonka climb up get to the button on the wall? Circle your answer.

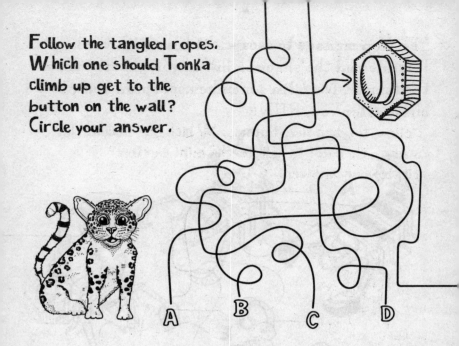

A   B   C   D

Solve the number problems and write the answers in the boxes at the end of the tangled lines. This will reveal the code for you to activate the lever!

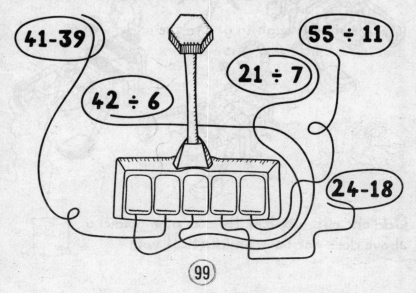

41-39

42 ÷ 6

21 ÷ 7

55 ÷ 11

24-18

Yes! You manage to escape the trap with your friends and the shapes... but as you get free from the temple, Mandra sends her scorpion army to chase after you. RUN!

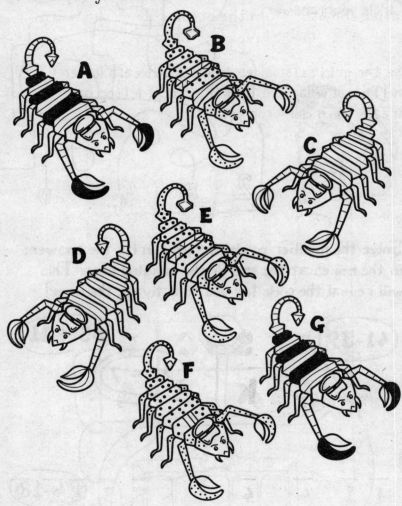

Odd one out: which of the scorpion soldiers above does not have an identical twin?

The scorpions chase you through the tunnels and down 1,000 steps, back to where the train dropped you off. Just when you think it's too late and the scorpions are gaining on you, you notice something on the other side of the train tracks that could save you!

Use the grid references to work out each letter and reveal what you find. The first letter has already been done for you.

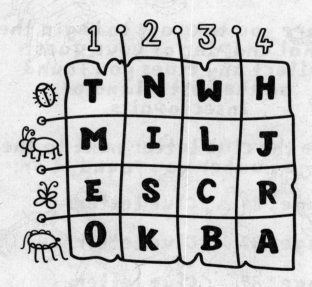

H _ _ _ _ _   _ _ _ _ _ _ _
4 1 1 4 2 4   3 4 3 3 1 1 2

CLUE LOGBOOK:
Insectopolis

Atlas the moth is the owner and captain of a large hot air balloon. They're happy to help you escape if they can join you, Jet, Tonka and Luca on your adventures!

Before you take off to begin the final chapter of your quest, collect any clues you found on the Lost Island of Insectopolis.

Note the clue letter next to the Page number you found it on:

Page : 84   Clue letter: ◯

Page : 87   Clue letter: ◯

Page : 89   Clue letter: ◯

Page : 90   Clue letter: ◯

Page : 96   Clue letter: ◯

★ NOTES ★

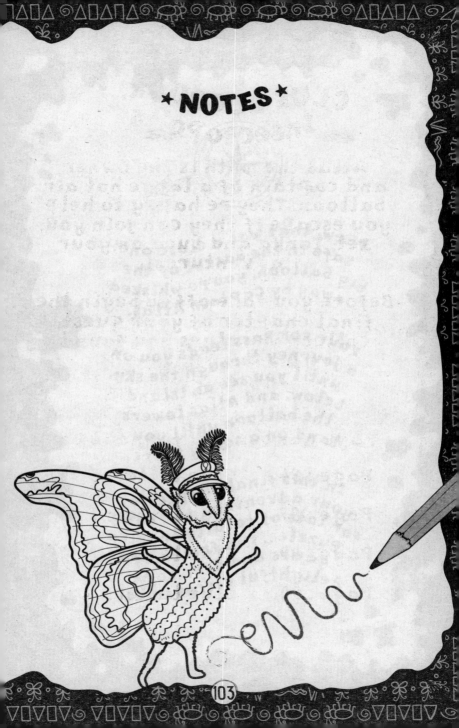

Phew, that was a close one!
Safe in the basket of the
big balloon, you're whisked
away by Captain Atlas.

Your compass leads you on
a journey through the sky,
until you see an island
below, and Atlas lowers
the balloon until you
land on a sandy shore.

In this final chapter of
your adventure, be ready
for lots of totally tropical
puzzles, fun fruit word
games and even some
delightful discoveries!

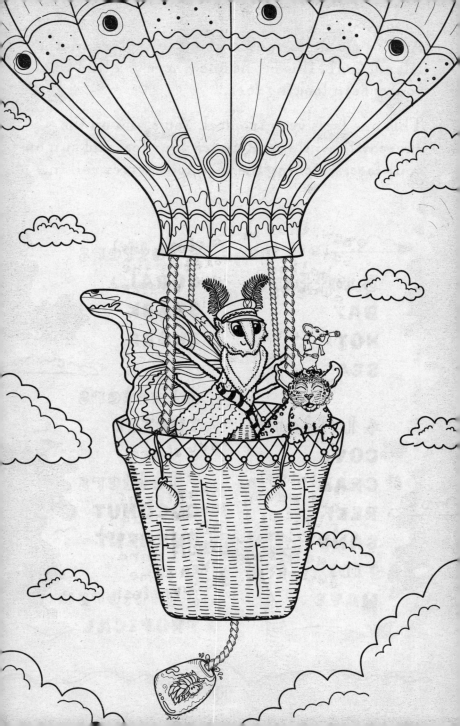

And so you find yourself about to explore another island. Could this be the one where you find what you've been looking for...?

This one feels very tropical. You stand on the shore with white sand under your feet and sun on your face, watching the turquoise waves roll in.

3 letters
BAY
HOT
SEA

4 letters
COVE
CRAB
REEF
SAND
TIDE
WAVE

5 letters
CORAL
SHARK
SHORE

6 letters
TURTLE

7 letters
COCONUT
CURRENT

8 letters
TROPICAL

Place each of the beach words from the list on the opposite page into the empty squares to create a filled crossword grid. Each word is used once so cross it off the list as you place it to help you keep track.

The first thing you notice when you start to explore the shore is how many crabs there are on this beach.

There are more crab species here on these sands than you've ever seen in your life!

COCONUT

FIDDLER

GHOST

HERMIT

HORSESHOE

RED KING

SHORE

SPIDER

Can you find all eight of the crab species from the
list on the opposite page in the wordsearch below?
Words may be hidden horizontally or vertically.

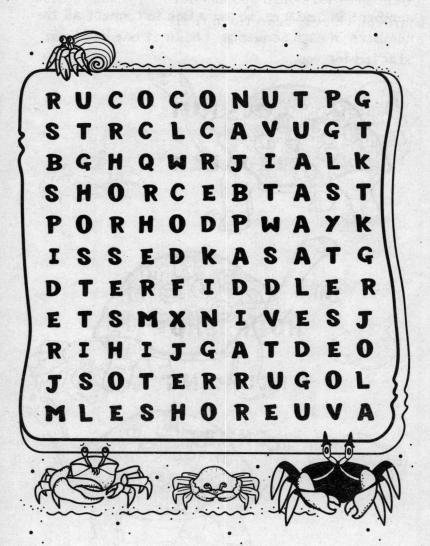

```
R U C O C O N U T P G
S T R C L C A V U G T
B G H Q W R J I A L K
S H O R C E B T A S T
P O R H O D P W A Y K
I S S E D K A S A T G
D T E R F I D D L E R
E T S M X N I V E S J
R I H I J G A T D E O
J S O T E R R U G O L
M L E S H O R E U V A
```

Wow! On the beach you also find some giant tortoises.

On each giant tortoise shell, look for a sequence or number pattern that connects the two white numbers in squares. Draw a line to connect all the numbers in each sequence. The first one has been started for you.

You'd think these giant reptiles had huge appetites, but they can actually go without food or drink for up to a year because they're so good at storing energy!

In the word-wheels, find three things that a giant tortoise might eat. Each word starts with the centre letter and uses all the letters in the wheel once.

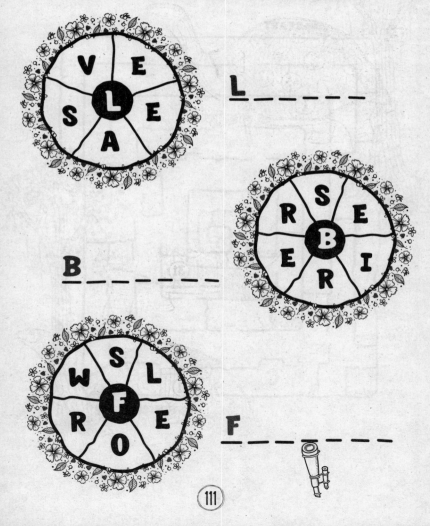

L _ _ _ _ _

B _ _ _ _ _ _

F _ _ _ _ _

As you walk inland from the beach, you find a
forest full of tall, spotted trees and twisted vines.

Can you make your way through the forest
maze from start to finish? Try not
to trip over any crooked roots!

START

FINISH!

As you look closer, you notice the forest is moving. It seems these trees are home to many weird and wonderful species of skink!

Make your way from start to finish. You can move up, down or sideways but you can't move diagonally and you must follow the skinks in this order:

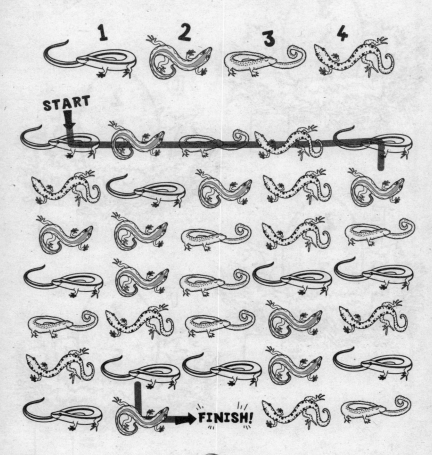

Further into the forest, you discover some nests on the ground... they're very big!

Complete the number problem in each egg and write your answers into the boxes. Each nest should have the same answer.

Which nest is the odd one out?

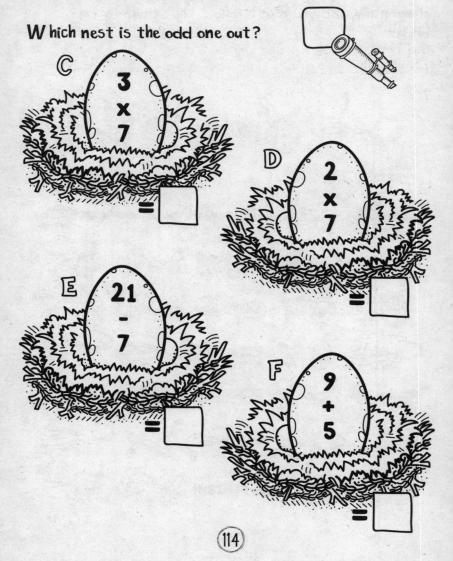

C

3
x
7

=

D

2
x
7

=

E

21
-
7

=

F

9
+
5

=

Hmm... these seem to be the ground nests of a very large kind of flightless bird thought to be extinct for over 300 years!

Could they really still be living here on this secret island after all this time?

Use the grid references to work out each letter and find out the name of the bird species. The first letter has already been done for you.

D __ __ __
4🐾 2🌴 3🥚 1⭐

≋ Yes, you've found them! ≋

While dodos have been thought of as extinct all this time, here on this island they have been secretly living and evolving, hidden away from the rest of the world.

Scribble out every letter F, K, P and X. Write the letters that are left over on the lines below to reveal a message from Mango the dodo. The first one has been done for you.

PWFEKLPCXOMFETKOP
DXODFOISKPLXAFNKD

W _ _ _ _ _ _ _

_ _ _ _

_ _ _ _ !

Can you solve the sudoku puzzle inside each set of dodo footprints?

The numbers 1, 2, 3 and 4 should be added to each row, each column and each 2x2 bold outlined box, but should only appear once in each one. The first one has been done for you.

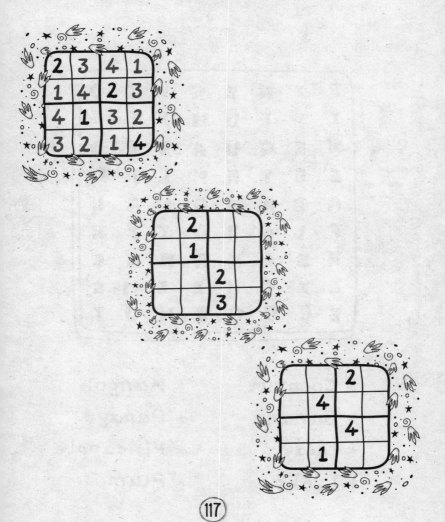

The dodos here are all named after different kinds of fruit that grow on this island.

Can you find all eight of their names in the wordsearch below? Words may be hidden in the grid horizontally or vertically.

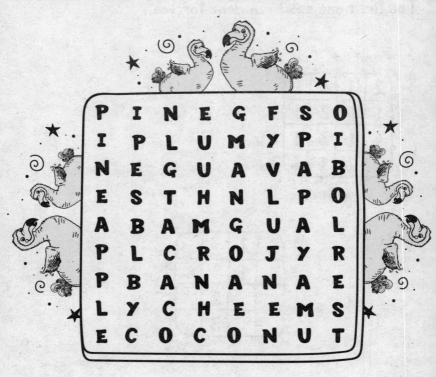

P	I	N	E	G	F	S	O
I	P	L	U	M	Y	P	I
N	E	G	U	A	V	A	B
E	S	T	H	N	L	P	O
A	B	A	M	G	U	A	L
P	L	C	R	O	J	Y	R
P	B	A	N	A	N	A	E
L	Y	C	H	E	E	M	S
E	C	O	C	O	N	U	T

★ Coconut
★ Banana
★ Guava
★ Lychee
★ Mango
★ Papaya
★ Pineapple
★ Plum

Woah, no one's ever seen dodos this tall before. Their legs are wildly long!

Follow the numbers from the dodos' feet and up their legs. Figure out which number is next in the sequence. Write the final number into the square in each dodo's body.

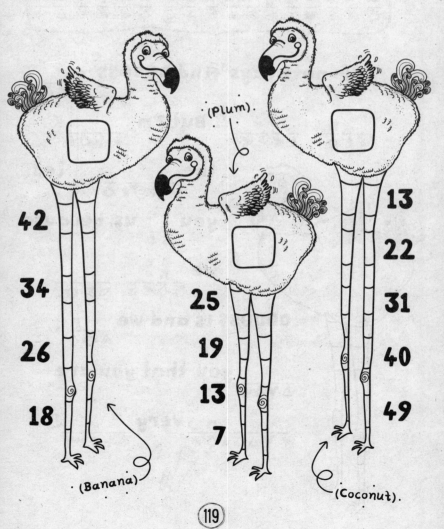

(Plum)

42
34
26
18
(Banana)

25
19
13
7

13
22
31
40
49
(Coconut).

You ask the dodos about the note, compass and map you found at the start of your adventure.

Use the symbol key to crack the code and fill in the gaps to reveal what Plum the dodo tells you.

a	c	d	e	f	g	h	i	k	l	m	n	o	p	s	t	w
✿	⋀	ē	▽	γ	✳	▷·	★	°⋄	❀	◎	◇	◄	⋇	米	△	◡

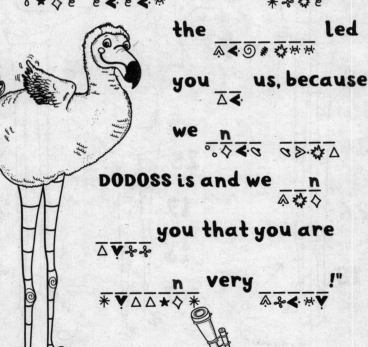

"The note says 'find DODOSS' **not**

'**find** **dodos**'. But I'm **glad**

the **compass** led

you **to** us, because

we **know** **what**

DODOSS is and we **can**

tell you that you are

getting very **close**!"

120

Plum says there's somewhere, just a little deeper into the forest, you need to visit to find out more...

Cross out any letter that appears more than once in the grid below. Write the letters that are left over on the lines below in the order they appear, and a hidden word will reveal itself. Letter **W** has been scribbled out to start you off.

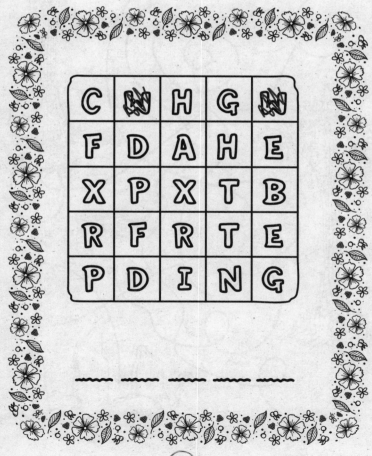

___ ___ ___ ___ ___

Plum tells you to follow the forest path that leads you all the way to the circle of stones.

Which of the tangled paths will take you there?

The stone in the centre of the circle has spaces for all six of the strange shapes you've been collecting on your journey.

Solve the number problem below each letter in the Key. Then use the answers to fill in the gaps and find out what happens when you place all of the shapes into the stone. One letter has been done for you.

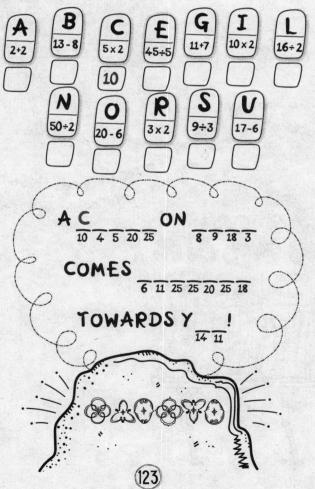

A	B	C	E	G	I	L
2+2	13-8	5×2	45÷5	11+7	10×2	16÷2
		10				

N	O	R	S	U
50÷2	20-6	3×2	9÷3	17-6

A C _ _ _ _ _ ON
  10 4 5 20 25   8 9 18 3

COMES _ _ _ _ _ _ _
       6 11 25 25 20 25 18

TOWARDS Y _ _ !
          14 11

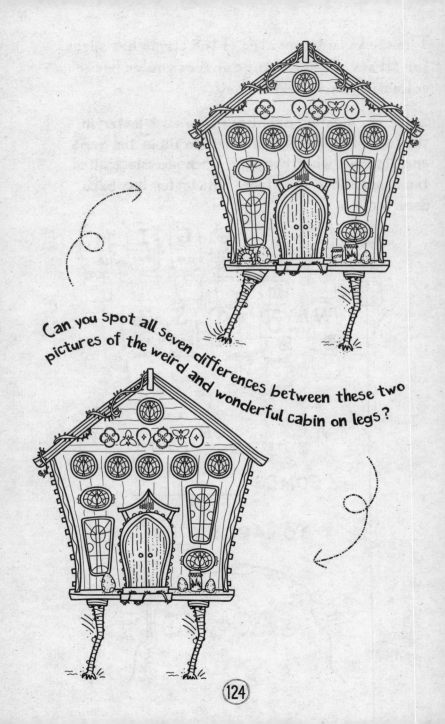

Can you spot all seven differences between these two pictures of the weird and wonderful cabin on legs?

You realise that the shapes you've been collecting are on the front of the cabin, and they have little letters inside them. Together, they spell 'DODOSS'.

Use the symbol key below to fill in the gaps and reveal what 'DODOSS' stands for. (Look closely, some of the shapes are quite similar!)

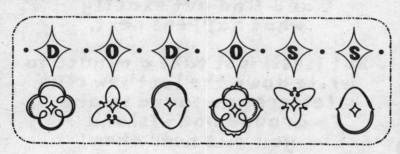

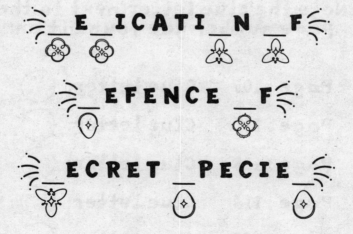

Hmm, interesting. The cabin lowers to the ground, and you step inside...

CLUE LOGBOOK:
Dodo Island

In a moment, you will continue
and find out exactly
what happens next.

But first, just take a minute to
write down the last few clue
letters you found in and
around Dodo Island
— you will need them!

Note the clue letter next to the
Page number you found it on:

Page : 107   Clue letter: ◯

Page : 111   Clue letter: ◯

Page : 114   Clue letter: ◯

Page : 116   Clue letter: ◯

Page : 120   Clue letter: ◯

★The story continues... ★

Inside the cabin, you are greeted by a very old dodo, who introduces themselves as 'The Keeper'.

The Keeper welcomes you to this hub for the 'Dedication of Defence of Secret Species', and congratulates you – you found DODOSS!

But there is something else you should know...

Crack the code on the next page to reveal the ending of the story.

Crack the code to finish the story!

Look back at all five Clue Logbooks on Pages 30, 54, 78, 102 and 126. Write the clue letters into the key below:

(For example, because you found the letter 'E' on Page 17, the letter 'E' is in the '17' box)

Once your key is complete, you can crack the code to reveal the story ending!

THE O_ K_____ OF D____
53 21 24 65 17 17 22 17 49   24 53 24 53 37 37

WILL BE R_____ SOON.
49 17 29 116 49 116 89 120

SOMEONE NEEDS TO TAKE O___
53 107 17 49

THE S_____ FOR MORE S_____
37 17 73 49 114 44   37 17 114 49 17 29

I_____ THEY WILL NEED TO
116 37 21 73 89 24 37

CONTINUE D_____ AND
24 116 37 114 53 107 17 49 116 89 120

P_____ ALL THE U_____
22 49 53 29 17 114 29 116 89 120   87 89 116 96 87 17

AND SECRET A_____ S_____
73 89 116 67 73 21   37 22 17 114 116 17 37

YOU WERE SENT ON THIS QUEST

TO SEE IF YOU H___ WHAT IT
44 73 107 17

T____ AND YOU P_____!
29 73 65 17 37   22 73 37 37 17 24

WILL YOU BECOME THE

N__ K_____ OF DODOSS?
89 17 111 65 17 17 22 17 49

Congratulations

You've completed your quest!
The adventure isn't over
just yet...

You'll find more Puzzle Quest fun
online at collins.co.uk/puzzlequest

But wait!

You'll need the secret password...

Use the key from page 128 to crack
the code and reveal your answer!

The secret password is

$$\overline{65} \quad \overline{17} \quad \overline{17} \quad \overline{22} \quad \overline{17} \quad \overline{49}$$

PUZZLE
Answers

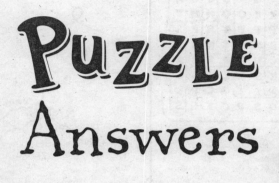

Pages 10 & 11 – Wordsearch

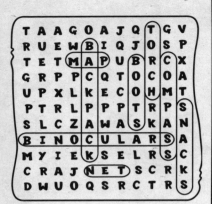

Page 13 – Tangled Paths

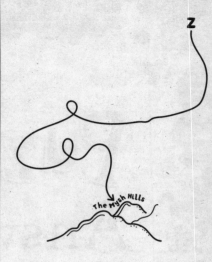

Page 12 – Silhouette Match

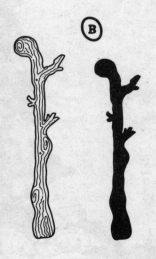

Page 14 – Maze

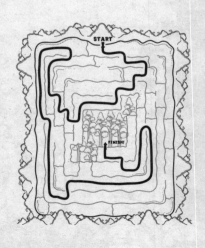

Page 15 – Code-Cracker

AS YOU ENTER THE
FOREST, YOU FIND
A STRANGE
SHAPE ON THE
GROUND. YOU DON'T
KNOW WHAT IT
IS, BUT IT FEELS
IMPORTANT SO
YOU PUT IT IN
YOUR BACKPACK.

A – 5	N – 8
B – 2	O – 15
C – 12	P – 14
D – 7	R – 18
E – 25	S – 3
H – 30	T – 10
M – 4	U – 6

Page 16 – Sudoku

4	3	1	2
1	2	4	3
2	1	3	4
3	4	2	1

1	2	3	4
4	3	2	1
2	1	4	3
3	4	1	2

2	4	3	1
3	1	4	2
4	2	1	3
1	3	2	4

Page 17 – Word-Wheels

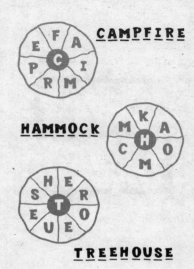

CAMPFIRE

HAMMOCK

TREEHOUSE

Page 18 – Spot the Difference

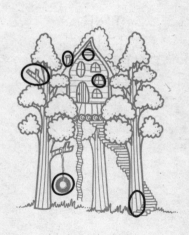

Page 19 – Order Game

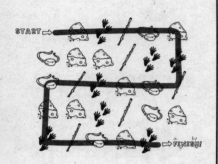

Page 20 – Word Scribble

JET
THE
EXPLORER
MOUSE

Page 21 – Word Tangle

Did you know that
  Mysh means mouse ?
What brought you
  to this tree house?
Our meeting was
  surely meant to be,
Exploring fills
  me up with glee!
Shall we let
  this story unravel?
May I come with
  you on your travels?

Page 22 – Code-Cracker

GRYLA THE GIANT
GOAT IS ANGRY THAT
YOU'RE IN THEIR
FOREST. YOUR
TREEHOUSE IS
GOING TO GET
KNOCKED OVER.
ESCAPE - QUICKLY!

Page 23 – Sequence Game

Page 24 – Maths Game

A $14 \times 3 = 42$

B $84 \div 2 = 42$

C $31 + 11 = 42$

D $25 + 9 = 34$

D is the odd one out

Page 25 – Sudoku

1	3	2	4
4	2	1	3
3	1	4	2
2	4	3	1

2	3	1	4
4	1	3	2
3	4	2	1
1	2	4	3

4	3	1	2
2	1	3	4
3	2	4	1
1	4	2	3

Pages 26 & 27 – Kriss Kross

135

Page 28 – Silhouette Match

Pages 34 – Maze

Page 29 – Wordfinder

BOAT

Page 35 – Wordfinder

IT LOOKS LIKE
THIS ISLAND IS
ONE HUGE
JUNGLE

```
      G   C
      R   A       V I N E   E
  R O S E W O O D       E
  A   N   P     W       R
  I   W   Y     A       G
  N   E       T E M P E R A T E   E
  F   T       A       M       E
  A   L A U R E L               N
  L       M O I S T
```

BEWARE!
TREE TERRORS
LIVE HERE!

1	4	2	3
3	2	4	1
2	1	3	4
4	3	1	2

2	4	1	3
3	1	2	4
4	2	3	1
1	3	4	2

3	2	4	1
4	1	3	2
1	4	2	3
2	3	1	4

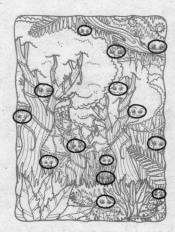

There are 14 Tree
Terrors watching you.

Page 41 – Sequence Game

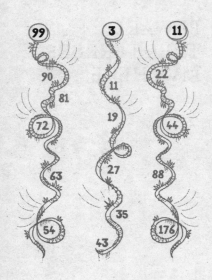

99 90 81 72 63 54

3 11 19 27 35 43

11 22 44 88 176

Page 42 – Odd One Out

The odd one out is X

Page 43 – Code-Cracker

"WE CAN HELP YOU IF YOU HELP US. THE CREATURES ON THE OTHER SIDE OF THE RIVER ARE SCARED OF US. WE ARE LONELY AND WOULD LIKE TO MAKE FRIENDS!"

A – 10   N – 20
D – 5   O – 16
E – 8   P – 15
H – 6   R – 3
I – 18   S – 9
K – 33   U – 13
L – 7   Y – 12

Page 44 – Tangled Paths

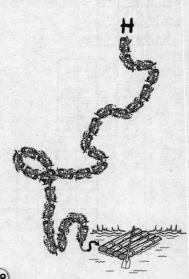

Page 45 – Code-Cracker

BEWARE!
TREE CHUMS
LIVE HERE

Page 48 – Silhouette Match

Pages 46 & 47 – Wordsearch

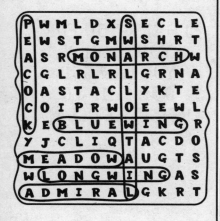

Page 49 – Word-Wheels

TIGER

JAGUAR

PANTHER

Page 50 – Code-Cracker

THE TREE CHUMS
ARE SO HAPPY
THEY HAVE LOTS
OF NEW FRIENDS
NOW! THEY INVITE
YOU AND THE
OTHER ANIMALS TO
A BIRTHDAY PARTY
IN THE JUNGLE.

Page 52 – Maths Game

A $6 \times 3 = 18$

B $38 \div 2 = 19$

C $54 \div 3 = 18$

D $15 + 3 = 18$

B is the odd one out

Page 51 – Order Game

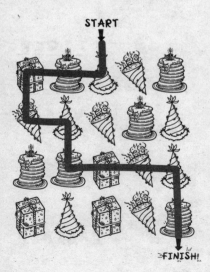

START

FINISH!

Page 53 – Word Scribble

THANK YOU FOR
YOUR HELP!
YOU CAN USE
OUR SHIP TO
CROSS THE OCEAN.

SUNKEN
ISLAND

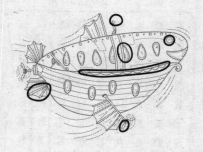

2	4	3	1
1	3	4	2
3	1	2	4
4	2	1	3

2	3	1	4
4	1	2	3
1	4	3	2
3	2	4	1

2	4	3	1
1	3	4	2
4	1	2	3
3	2	1	4

D

Page 62 – Wordfinder

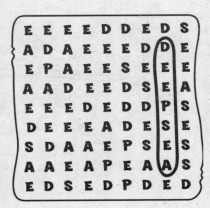

```
E E E E D D E D S
A D A E E E D D E
E P A E E S E E E
A A D E E D S E A
E E E D E D D P S
D E E E A D E S E
S D A A E P S E S
A A E A P E A A S
E D S E D P D E D
```

Pages 64 & 65 – Kriss Kross

```
                L
    S C A L L O P
    H         B     J
    A   M U S S E L
  C R A B     T     L     D
    K         T E E L Y   O
            T   R     Y F L
            U         I P
          S T A R F I S H I N
            L         S H
  W H A L E           H     N
```

Page 63 – Silhouette Match

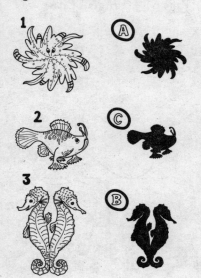

Page 66 – Maze

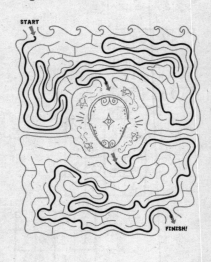

142

JUST AFTER YOU COLLECT THE SHAPE, A FLURRY OF SWIMMING SEA SLUGS COME ALONG AND STEAL IT!

A – 9	N – 10
E – 1	R – 8
F – 20	S – 18
G – 4	T – 7
I – 13	U – 3
L – 27	W – 11
M – 5	Y – 15

D

The odd one out is D

YOU CAN HAVE THE SHAPE IF YOU CALM THE CATFISH

Page 72 – Order Game

Page 73 – Code-Cracker

TOOTHACHE

Page 74 – Tangled Paths

Page 75 – Word Tangle

"I must thank thee
  for setting me free
That tooth and I,
  did not agree.
I'm now happy
  to eat algae...
Sorry sea slugs,
I'll leave you be! "

Page 76 – Order Game

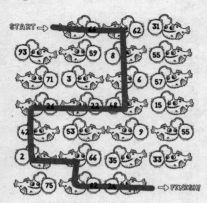

Page 82 – Anagrams

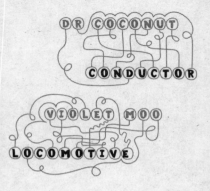

Page 77 – Maths Game

A 16 x 2 = 32

B 60 - 26 = 34

C 12 + 22 = 34

D 17 x 2 = 34

A is the odd one out

Page 83 – Word-Wheels

STEAM

ENGINE

TRACKS

ALL ABOARD
THE CREEPY
CRAWLER!

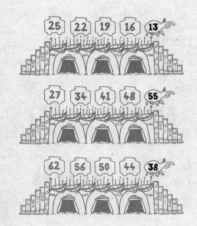

Page 93 – Sudoku

4	2	3	1
1	3	2	4
2	1	4	3
3	4	1	2

1	2	3	4
4	3	2	1
3	4	1	2
2	1	4	3

3	4	1	2
1	2	4	3
2	1	3	4
4	3	2	1

Page 94 – Order Game

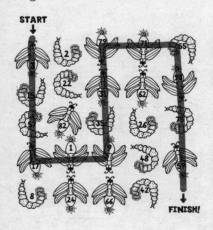

Page 95 – Wordsearch

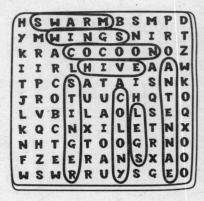

Pages 96 & 97 – Code-Cracker

IN THE THRONE ROOM, YOU MEET QUEEN MANDRA THE MANTIS. SHE SAYS SHE HAD A VISION THAT TOLD HER SHE "SHOULD GIVE YOU THE SHAPES AND LET YOU GO". SO, SHE GIVES YOU TWO MORE SHAPES... BUT, AS YOU TURN TO LEAVE, MANDRA SAYS, "ALAS, I DON'T BELIEVE IN VISIONS ANY MORE!" SHE PUSHES A BUTTON AND THE FLOOR OPENS UP! UH OH! YOU, JET, TONKA AND LUCA FALL DEEP DOWN INTO A TRAP! NOW YOU ARE ALL STUCK. THAT WAS UNEXPECTED...

A – 8	O – 13
D – 7	P – 16
E – 20	Q – 18
H – 9	R – 15
I – 44	S – 30
L – 5	T – 6
M – 4	U – 10
N – 3	V – 12

Page 98 – Tangled Paths

Page 99 – Tangled Paths and Code-Cracker

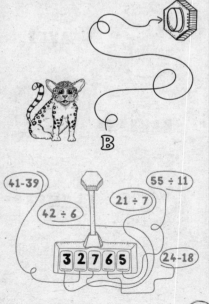

Page 100 – Odd One Out

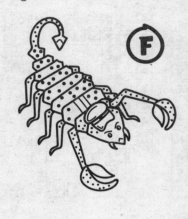

Page 101 – Code-Cracker

HOT AIR BALLOON

Pages 106 & 107 – Kriss Kross

```
    T   R         H O T
C U R R E N T         I D
O     O   E         R   I D
V     P   F     S H O R E
E     I   A             E
      C O C O N U T
S E A     O   D     U
S H A R K O   R     C R A B
H     A   L   R     T
A       B A Y       T
R       L           L
K         W A V E   E
```

Page 110 – Sequence Game

Ⓐ Ⓑ Ⓒ

Pages 108 & 109 – Wordsearch

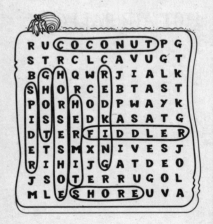

Page 111 – Word-Wheels

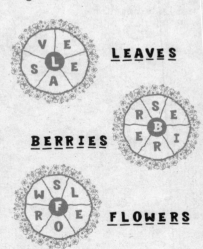

LEAVES

BERRIES

FLOWERS

Page 112 – Maze

Page 113 – Order Game

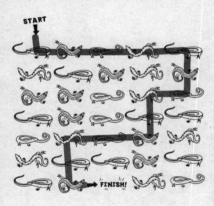

Page 114 – Maths Game

C   **3 x 7 = 21**

D   **2 x 7 = 14**

E   **21 - 7 = 14**

F   **9 + 5 = 14**

C is the odd one out

Page 115 – Code-Cracker

DODO

Page 116 – Word Scribble

WELCOME TO DODO ISLAND!

Page 118 – Wordsearch

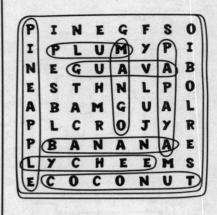

```
P  I  N  E  G  F  S  O
I  P  L  U  M  y  P  I
N  E  G  U  A  V  A  B
E  S  T  H  N  L  P  O
A  B  A  M  G  U  A  L
P  L  C  R  O  J  y  R
P  B  A  N  A  N  A  E
L  y  C  H  E  E  M  S
E  C  O  C  O  N  U  T
```

Page 117 – Sudoku

```
2  3  4  1
1  4  2  3
4  1  3  2
3  2  1  4
```

```
4  2  1  3
3  1  4  2
1  3  2  4
2  4  3  1
```

```
1  3  2  4
2  4  1  3
3  2  4  1
4  1  3  2
```

Page 119 – Sequence Game

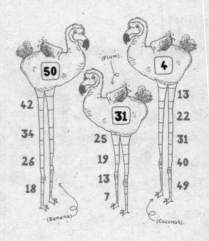

50

(Plum)

31

4

42   13
34   25   22
26   19   31
18   13   40
       7   49

(Banana)   (Coconut)

"The note says 'find DODOSS' not 'find dodos'. But I'm glad the compass led you to us, because we know what DODOSS is and we can tell you that you are getting very close! "

CABIN

A CABIN ON LEGS COMES RUNNING TOWARDS YOU!

A – 4	L – 8
B – 5	N – 25
C – 10	O – 14
E – 9	R – 6
G – 18	S – 3
I – 20	U – 11

DEDICATION OF DEFENCE OF SECRET SPECIES

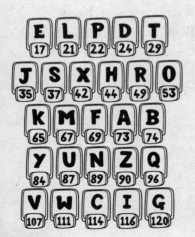

THE OLD KEEPER OF DODOSS WILL BE RETIRING SOON.

SOMEONE NEEDS TO TAKE OVER THE SEARCH FOR MORE SECRET ISLANDS. THEY WILL NEED TO CONTINUE DISCOVERING AND PROTECTING ALL THE UNIQUE AND SECRET ANIMAL SPECIES.

YOU WERE SENT ON THIS QUEST TO SEE IF YOU HAVE WHAT IT TAKES AND YOU PASSED!

WILL YOU BECOME THE NEW KEEPER OF DODOSS?

★ NOTES ★

✴ NOTES ✴

(Blank 'notes' pages like this are handy for jotting down any notes or working out when you're busy solving puzzles!

You could also use them to write, doodle, or anything else you'd like while on your quest!)

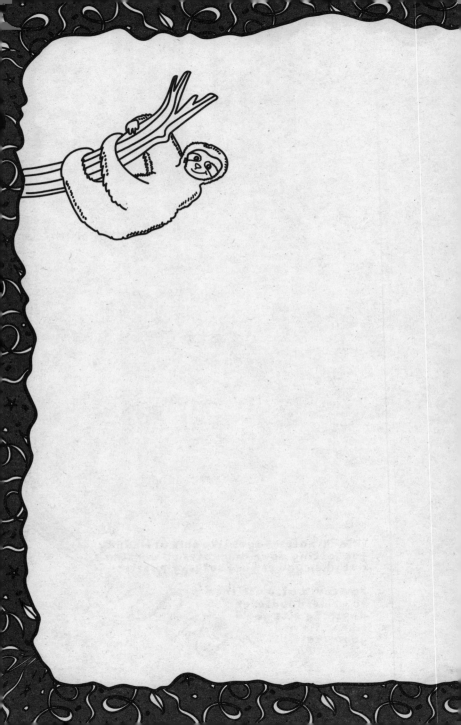

★NOTES★

⋆ NOTES ⋆